I0146886

Dark Fish and the Sermon
of St. Anthony

Dark Fish and the Sermon of St. Anthony

By
Erica Maria Litz

Joy is Free, LLC Publishing
Tempe, Arizona
2017©
info@joyisfree.org

Copyright Erica Maria Litz © 2017. All rights reserved.

No part of this book may be used or reproduced in any manner whatsoever without the prior written permission of the copyright owner.

Cover photo © 2017 by Erica Maria Litz. All rights reserved.
Cover design by Erica Maria Litz

ISBN: 978-0692877050

Published by Joy is Free, LLC Publishing, Tempe, Arizona
joyisfree.org

Books by Erica Maria Litz

Lightning Forest, Lava Root Published by Plain View Press 2009

for Iria and Joseph

Love and dance this world, my loves. Pray and laugh to the end.

Dark Fish and the Sermon
of St. Anthony

"There is geometry in the humming of the strings, music in

the spacing of the spheres."

— Pythagoras

Strange Bend

I told the children the world has a strange bend in the oddest of

places.

The poor beast contorts time while one woman works ten hours a

day, and the new gal

gets paid full-time to work five. The beautiful beast bends the air

into jagged

twine around the airways of the asthmatic. Her pain. Her grief, all a

tangle.

Strange bends in the sound waves warp the mind of lost, stolen,

consumed lives—

decapitated children, hacked identities, the lies.

I told the children. Know it's there, the strange bend.

You must know, see, that you can dance around it, breathe deep and

dive under

the bending air, the storm overhead. Dance around and know

laughter

bends strange openings to safe passages. Laugh and force open the

airways—the cough passes.

Strange bends in the mind, for those, pray and be still.

Look, see the beautiful beast during the worst bending. Look to that

moment—it still holds hidden, encapsulated joy in the song of a

peach-faced lovebird or the dove

that shits on your mother's head on Mother's Day. Laugh

at the strange bends.

Pray them away from the children. Love the beautiful

beast. See. Listen to the bird in the minutes of sorrow. Let the desert

willow's sway

silence the roaring bend of stress. Watch for the beautiful beast.

With these things,

you can take her.

I.

some times an ionic disturbance

lights up the upper atmosphere

knocks out the grid

do we remember after

teeth rattle to the floor

boil the water

which shrub is for tea

can the children clean a fish

do they know the food around them

can they grow more

will it

be enough

II

rainbow bombs

missiles tear the midnight sacred space

man-made auroras

radioactive particles in the sky

while men mine anti-protons from the belts

III.

sonic weapons manipulate plasma

situational awareness at 10 years old

a boy and his mother wonder

how to prepare a young man for such things

IV.

we walk to hear the dirt and gravel

settle our feet to earth

draw out the confusion

step down on fear

we can see a ring 'round the moon

a promise

we'll smell the greasewood on the breeze

morning's right

my babies

painite and platinum

V.

we found a spring

away from nanotalk

mom's worry of the future

how the waves may hit

no way to ride them

bent to cup the water

she holds it well

VI.

unheld for a decade

untouched for years

her brown wolf comforts

lets her fingertips know his ears

no thieves returning

no silver left to steal

her hands are thick and rough

nails short and steeled

soil musks her palms

settles in the crevices

VII.

a woman turns to brew tea

bougainvillea to calm the cough

her daughter with asthma wheezes while awake

sings melodies in her sleep

VIII.

russian pine and ponderosa

sap and sap

nut and nuts

but survival is the crooked forest of gryfino

IX.

neptune flaunts his new high pressure vortex

with ever bright companion cloud

unfaithful

where is the eye for her own cirrus

his steady rise to cumulus

the joy in his familiar scent in the air

X.

50% of a lot is still a lot

what friend advises a mother to spend

her savings to gravel the yard

recession ends but must

the children eat stones

XI.

roast pig on a spit

give the choicest to those

damned determined to take

the heads of our children

let them eat their own

XII.

chimera tortured in glass chambers

the degreed cannibals harvest for the greater

none loved

locked in the unnatural

Lord have mercy on our souls

we know and yet what we don't do

XIII.

a forgotten intentional loss for a generation ill—

informed against that which frees

put on a smile agreeable

owned for velvet lies of security

unified in trust of standby

find the papers

forget the ink

the court officials will arrive

XIV.

medicine so good in meadows is on TV

fine print flitters about

a bleeding tongue

the inability to move when waking

erection with blindness

suicidal thoughts

clear sinus

XV.

a treatise on an owl and a dark figure

turned down the alley—seen by a child

who sees what is out of ordinary

wise, he prays

and the demon

must fall

XVI.

caravans roll north

escape in nissans

we take the hidden pass

our friends let us through

high beyond the desert

where we trust

a well of sweet water

and bear the sore

breasts of a new cycle

XVII.

we have water here

mars can keep his in his pants

far away from the wallets of the people

remembering the dance in the rain

the knee bone of St. Anthony

safe and entombed below

the silk painting of a peach tree

we have that

XVIII.

science hints at magnetoreception

what we once called perspicacia

the knowing that doesn't come from books

a trust some lost

XIX.

Some days are everything hot with the frothed milk

extra cinnamon powder and a shot of espresso

please

bacon sandwich that

thank you

XX.

optogenetics and neurological enhancers—the new fiefdom

sold souls no longer elevated by grit

can't buy the crispiest design

no more time to aspire

cipher to life the undead executive

XXI.

stay eyes up toward the moon

harvest the corn when it wanes

read psalms at its fullest

feet firm to the ground

don't trust the black lily

XXII.

unable to decipher this code

broken dashes

the shadow marks innocuous on a pale wall

XXIII.

meaning over math

codes over ciphers

syntax reigns over algorithm

sometimes

you will be told the contrary

Habukkuk

but yet there is the divine

geometry

XXIV.

drop it into the mind age

xenotransplantation—solicit is spelled wrong on

the whiteboard

blank and begging

meaning from a squeal

drawn out

XXV.

milo is still plenty

we forgot the water,

earth, gas, and sun alchemy

condemn the man who protects

his hands worn and mind splintered at the cost

the how long the earth pushed to bring that fruit

to bear

XXVI.

how did fire appropriate what wasn't primary to it

lift its leg and piss on what it didn't give up or build

fire fanned by full noises

its orange too bored to wait for the hands of clay

too bored to form a brick and use its heat to strengthen it

to make it

to build something for itself

XXVII.

a continental rebuke to all this royal noise

the buzz and clicks of progress

turn to bash and shrill

the whine—all the searching

turns to non-noise madness

XXVIII.

today, winter started

it's gone so far

it's too far

quaint lines really

we must plant

out of the pot

into the ground

we must plant

before the season passes

XXIX.

maybe a cat runs his rough tongue

across the coat of man

until it scratches away the fine

hairs of humanness

those fine hairs of sense

XXX.

for God's sake

how does one

strip and re-caulk

the tub

without tearing it up

or needing

a new one

XXXI.

a ten-year old

son sees his mother

his sole parent

struggle with a scraper

desperate to make clean,

make beautiful

what he and his sister need

and chooses

again

to step up

to help

more man than man

he makes use of the old

XXXII.

when all else is spun into lost

we will make a fire

roast cicada,

find some stale

marshmallows,

and thank God over the water sip,

eyes up to the stars

XXXIII.

in the morning, do you know

a daughter

sharpens her knife

cooks a fish

boils water

reads

prays

sings over firelight

XXXIV.

some ends are worse than others

all frayed, singed twine

we don't really all suffer the same

what is telling

is the how

one suffers the peels of life

how

one rises, takes the shattered ends

off the linoleum floor

flexes the jaw back into place

glues the gash in the chin closed,

and rebraids nerves, flesh, hair back to

lift a child to hip and hobble

right out that flimsy door

XXXV.

a villain in the midst

unseen and tangled black

like lace slid over

the thigh of this place

crept in the underseen

XXXVI.

wind in the sonora

signals the coming of dry

grit in teeth

dust

or hope of rain to come

desert children

avoid umbrellas

dance mud

let the storms fall

bless them

desert children

don't need to hide

feet from puddles

shoulders from warm precipitation

desert children know

home isn't

just dust

they celebrate

every drop with a run

a dance

a splash of delight

XXXVII.

nails and needles

in the headlines

in candy bars

again

seriously

WTH

      children

      candy

      needles

      and nails

not the fairytale

villain's spell

we knew before

      not new

but a twist

      another twist

in the world that fell

      hard to nails

wrists to tree

XXXVIII.

grandma needled

fine threaded crochet

she edged her linens

with prayers

her bedding

with stars

what magic

in her hands

what patient conjuring

of light

trims her children's homes

with the intricate

universes

she made all around us

XXXIX.

when ballistic missile

is a headline

it's time

to bake something

clean anything

or

take grandma

and grandpa

to lunch

it's time to call

aunts

time to live

and water the roses

they're dying again

save them

neglect the chores

go

take the kids to a movie

on a hike

the far off

fiends

are at it again

XXXX.

I have decided

I've decided

too much

please

no more

deciding

to decide

more

living

to live

with imperfect curves

and messy turns

unfinished

homework

and half-eaten words

let's burn

report cards

their templates

let's just learn

for its own sake

let's stare at stars

learn their names

let's tell stories

and call them games, wonders

and dig

a row

wander in fields

find bugs

find stones

look things up

from the earth

roll them

in our palms

let's take tests

and delete them

let's revel in success

and progress with doodled ~

listening to know

what actually sticks

stays in the mind

with curved lines

flowers

and funny faces

but

not forgotten

tell the fools

it's not idealism

it's true

read the science

XXXXI.

could someone share

with scientists

not all

just the ones

who forgot

we don't live

in a comic book

I love them

scientists

but really

chimera

sad

lonely

lacerated

chimera

eviscerated

tortured cousin

of man

XXXXII.

we slapped each other

with cabbage leaves

laughed

we didn't ponder

the fractal nature

halved

just amazed

laughed again

we shocked

sister into shaking

her head

at weirdness she loves

XXXXIII.

when a son of four

says mom

you don't have to

put the ugly words

in between the other words

you can just

leave them out

it's best to abide

or at least

thank him

and laugh at one's own

ridiculous attempts

at broken emphasis

XXXXIV.

she may have

blown off

every

single

chore

twice

but when she runs to you, mother

to the quiet car

tells you her secret

at thirteen

trusts

hungry for your guidance

bite your tongue

until it bleeds

make your ears soft

and large

breathe steady

speak softly

she told you

she asked for advice

about a big thing

and won

XXXXV.

too many tabs open

too many plates

spin

poetry

turns

to telegraphing

a line

escapes

the noise

escapes the buzz

gets through

from too much

heavy metal to ethereal

something or other

the water bill

the other bill

which

that fax

no one uses

but is required

yes

a line

escapes

through the PhD

edit the novel

by someone

the dryer

fold

feed

a line

to page

whispers in the crowd

XXXXVI.

a dream of chinchillas

sounds soft, warm

but they are

endangered

they were

everywhere

in all the trees

had small hutches

odd

in my parent's backyard

a friend suggests

I may lack warmth in my life

a partner

to caress

maybe

but I hope

that one

is not

related to rats

XXXXVII.

I insist

Roman numerals

assert titles in tidy numerals

all angular

sharp

but regular

pretty patterns of officialdom

almost stamps

of here-starts-another

leak from the ethos

I mean ether

shit

no firmament

empyrean

ah

sexy

no leaked empyreal here

nonsense

still single

XXXXVIII.

my country

tis

in a shitstorm

love you

still love

love now

we have it

we

have

it

better together

than apart

hold to the can part

hold to the Am part

we the people

have words

have love

words to turn to love

XXXXIX.

I in a room full

of x's

in my head

that's all

at 12:32 AM

even

the coffee

has run

dry

lost its strength too

yet it was

something in the chill

and empty

L.

can a cry

follow five

Roman tens as x's

and stitches in the chin

after a fall

to linoleum

at a large man's feet

the feel of the jaw

extending

the side of the face

amazing in elasticity

yes scarred

not broken

LI.

"ancient sloths

ate mormon tea

and saltbush"

know that

Citation: Greggel, Laura, "Mummified Poop Reveals Ancient Sloth

Ate Mormon Tea and Saltbush." *LiveScience.* 1 November 2016.

LII.

ah, the pitch and rhythm of proteins

turning auditory representations

for researchers to hear their folding

false god songs mimic creation

and first there was the Word

He sings over us

counts the hairs of every

will turn the melody back

to the coming new

life, the dark fish

the right frequency

will heal

LIII.

understand the beautiful geometry

the basal song of the sea

of the aurora borealis

diffracted sound around us

we sense the strange bends

the warning of shofar

reverberated through our marrow

long enough to set us on a better course

a sounding laugh at fear

About the Author

Erica Maria Litz is a poet. Her first poetry collection, *Lightning Forest, Lava Root* was published by Plain View Press and is available in print and Kindle formats on Amazon at *Lightning Forest, Lava Root* by Erica Maria Litz

To contact the author, email Joy is Free, LLC Publishing at info@joyisfree.org

www.ingramcontent.com/pod-product-compliance
Lightning Source LLC
Chambersburg PA
CBHW072148090426
42739CB00013B/3317